Thank you to my family, without whom the sentiments and ideas upon which these words are based would not exist.

And to you, for sharing in them.

For Logan and Reese. My little planets.

They say many things about outer space
and its great expanse from place to place.
Its size and scope you can hardly dream.
To think of it may often seem
a daunting task, but if you try
it is quite marvelous. I'll tell you why.

Beneath this stillness beyond knowing
lies a world of miracles, moving and growing.

Spread in that boundless
tract of dark silk
lies a galaxy of
glittering spilt milk.
A grand spiral of
twinkling lights
spanning the
furthest depths
and heights.

And this
celestial
milky way is
twisting gently
day by day.
A trillion specks
of light and one...

...is our bright
and shining sun.

Around it float planets
through the fray
in great big ovals
as if for play.

Some small and hot.

Some big and cold.

Some with rings.　Some blue.

Some old.

In that crowd is
our very own earth,
the home that we all
share from birth.
Rotating around
the sun each year,
365 days if you're
counting here.

And spinning like a top too,
that's 24 hours to me and you.

On that earth lies the sea,
covering two-thirds of what we can see.

Pulled back and forth by the moon,
making tides in a surging tune.

Shifting softly to and fro,
in constant motion, on the go.

In that sea swims
a majestic whale,
splashing the surface with its tail.

The largest animal gets its fill
by feeding on the tiny krill.

For even the greatest being could not live
without the help the smallest give.

Beneath that whale dances a crab,
looking for a snack to grab.
Cutting across the floor like a knife,
its spindly legs kick up life.

Stretching for something
beyond its reach
as it makes its way
towards the beach

On that beach lies
a grain of sand...

...a miniature galaxy in the palm of your hand.

Thousands drifting through your fingers
into the sea in which they linger.
These tiny worlds form a vast array
to make the land on which you play.

And as your toes
   grip the sand
      of the beach
         on the land...

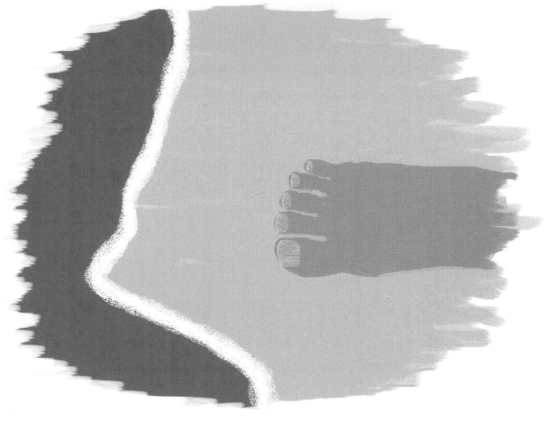

As the water
     from the sea
          laps your hand and
               knocks sand free...

As the sea
    gently glides
        building worlds
            with its tides...

As the earth
circles the sun
in its curving
yearly run...

Yes, in this constant universe of motion
with size and scope beyond wildest notion,
among the galaxies great and small...

...beats a heart.

The grandest thing of all.

It helps you drift from sea to sand and dance about with pail in hand.

It helps you swim, strong and brave, shifting with a cresting wave.

It helps you spin in the setting sun in constant floating, twisting fun.

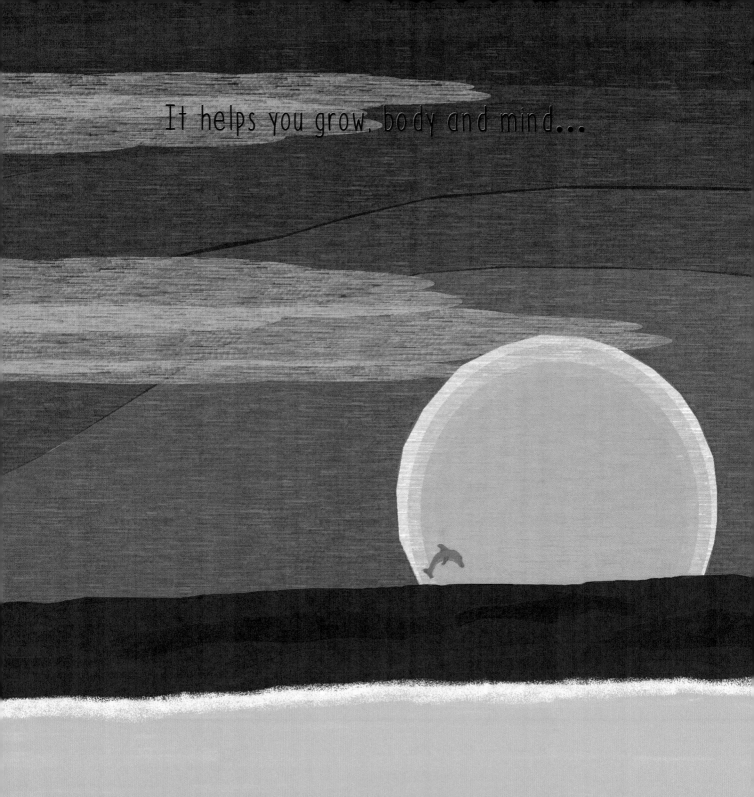

It helps you grow, body and mind...

...even as you sit,
still and kind.

So when you gaze upon the stars,
I hope you marvel at how grand they are,
knowing that, just like you,
they are dancing wonders,
through and through.

And when I consider the spinning awe
with breadth enough to drop the jaw,

I'll rest assured of my greatest notion....

You!

My little planet in constant motion.